Pebble™ Plus

Bugs, Bugs, Bugs!

Crickets

by Margaret Hall

Consulting Editor: Gail Saunders-Smith, PhD
Consultant: Gary A. Dunn, MS, Director of Education
Young Entomologists' Society Inc.
Lansing, Michigan

Capstone press

Mankato, Minnesota

Pebble Plus is published by Capstone Press
151 Good Counsel Drive, P.O. Box 669, Mankato, Minnesota 56002
www.capstonepress.com

1 2 3 4 5 6 09 08 07 06 05 04

Library of Congress Cataloging-in-Publication Data
Hall, Margaret, 1947–
    Crickets/by Margaret Hall.
    p.cm.—(Pebble plus: Bugs, bugs, bugs!)
    Includes bibliographical references and index.
    ISBN 0-7368-2587-8 (hardcover)
    1. Crickets—Juvenile literature. [1. Crickets.] I. Title. II. Series.
QL508.G8 H35 2005
595.7'26—dc22   2003024963

Summary: Simple text and photographs describe the physical characteristics and habits of crickets.

Editorial Credits
Sarah L. Schuette, editor; Linda Clavel, series designer; Kelly Garvin, photo researcher; Karen Hieb,
    product planning editor

Photo Credits
Bill Johnson, 20–21
Bruce Coleman Inc./Carol Hughes, 17; David C. Rentz, 18–19; Janis Burger, 11; John Shaw, 15;
    Raymond Tercafs, 4–5
David Liebman, 1, 12–13
Dwight R. Kuhn, cover
James P. Rowan, 8–9
Robert McCaw, 7

Note to Parents and Teachers

The Bugs, Bugs, Bugs! series supports national science standards related to the diversity of life and heredity. This book describes and illustrates crickets. The images support early readers in understanding the text. The repetition of words and phrases helps early readers learn new words. This book also introduces early readers to subject-specific vocabulary words, which are defined in the Glossary section. Early readers may need assistance to read some words and to use the Table of Contents, Glossary, Read More, Internet Sites, and Index/Word List sections of the book.

Word Count: 89
Early-Intervention Level: 11

Table of Contents

Crickets

What are crickets? Crickets
are insects that leap.

5

How Crickets Look

Most crickets have black,
green, or brown bodies.

7

Crickets are about the size
of a lima bean.

Crickets have six long legs.

They jump and hop.

Crickets have sharp jaws.

Jaws help crickets bite
and chew.

Crickets have two antennas.

Antennas help crickets feel

and smell.

What Crickets Do

Crickets hide during
the day. They come out
at night to eat.

Male crickets chirp. They rub their wings together to make chirping sounds.

Crickets listen to each
other. They have ears
on their legs.

Glossary

antenna—a feeler; crickets use antennas to sense movement and to smell

insect—a small animal with a hard outer shell, six legs, three body sections, and two antennas; most insects have wings.

jaw—a part of the mouth used to grab, bite, and chew

male—an animal that can father young

Read More

Jacobs, Liza. *Crickets.* Wild Wild World. San Diego: Blackbirch Press, 2003.

Meister, Cari. *Crickets.* Insects. Edina, Minn.: Abdo, 2001.

Squire, Ann O. *Crickets and Grasshoppers.* A True Book. New York: Children's Press, 2003.

Internet Sites

FactHound offers a safe, fun way to find Internet sites related to this book. All of the sites on FactHound have been researched by our staff.

Here's how:

1. Visit *www.facthound.com*

2. Type in this special code **0736825878** for age-appropriate sites. Or enter a search word related to this book for a more general search.

3. Click on the **Fetch It** button.

FactHound will fetch the best sites for you!

Index/Word List